THE BOOMER'S GUIDE to AGING PARENTS,

Volume Two, How to Choose a Home Care Worker

Carolyn L. Rosenblatt, RN, BSN, PHN, Attorney

"Practical Advice And Useful Tips To Help Avoid Common Pitfalls In Caring For Aging Parents"

AgingParents.com

You are not alone

The Boomer's Guide to Aging Parents: Volume Two,
Carolyn L. Rosenblatt, RN, BSN, PHN, Attorney

Table of Contents

Introduction

This book did not start out to be a book. It started with people asking questions. I retired from my litigation practice in 2007, after 29 years on the legal battlefield, as a litigator and trial lawyer. I had already taken several kinds of mediation training, and was beginning to do mediations. Sometimes people had a conflict, which needed dispute resolution services, but more often, they had questions about aging parents and relatives.

I had set out to do mediation (dispute resolution) for elders in elder care facilities, or wherever they were, so my focus was already on elders. I found myself answering questions more than mediating. It was interesting that so many questions were about the law, and how it interfaced with the healthcare issues of aging loved ones: elder abuse, assisted living facilities, contracts, family fights, who should take care of mom, and lots of other issues that were generating questions from clients and their families.

As a result, my consulting practice was born. What is satisfying for me is being able to use both nursing knowledge and legal knowledge in the same conversation with a client. It took eight years to get both of those degrees and many more years to get enough experience in both fields to be able to figure out what people needed to know. I feel deeply honored to be able to use the combined forty years of experience I have to be of assistance to anyone.

What I have observed is that people who are caring for aging parents do not face just one problem with those parents. Aging brings with it multiple problems for the caregivers. Some are health related. Some are emotional. Some are legal. Some are a combination. Usually, they are all mixed together in some way. My background seemed like a very good fit to be of service to those doing the sometimes very difficult job of caregiver.

I work with my husband, Dr. Mikol Davis, a clinical psychologist with over thirty years' experience, in consulting work and mediations. Particularly in working with families in conflict, his input is invaluable. He encouraged me to write things down, as so much helpful information comes from our clients. The writing seemed to grow and grow. Before I knew it, one volume led to another, until there were nine, with more to come.

My hope is that this book will relieve a little pressure, bring a little clarity, give some practical, hands-on advice, and help you, to have a better understanding of how the law, knowledge about the healthcare system, and common sense can help you get through this time. My husband and I are baby boomers, too. For all of us, this caretaking time is a new era in our lives. My wish for you is that you feel some support from your fellow boomer author.

When an aging parent or other loved one starts to lose the ability to do everyday things alone, such as bathing or cooking, the elder or her family may consider getting a helper. There may be resistance to the idea of help initially. For some elders, having to rely on a helper for anything is stressful and threatening. It can have a symbolic meaning, that "I'm going downhill" or "becoming a burden." Many elders resist "having a stranger in my house."

However, when the effects of aging prevent a loved one from managing his or her daily life alone, it is time to find out if help at home can solve the problem. The arena of home care workers is largely unregulated by government and by society in general. It is usually considered a private matter, which it is. The difficulty is that many people hire someone to work in the home on their own (without using an agency), and in doing so, they take more risks than they may realize.

This volume is an effort to educate adult children of aging parents, or the parents themselves, of the danger in hiring home care workers, especially without the help of an agency. It is also a guide to assist you through the process, giving you information about what to expect and how to do the hiring in a legal way.

As technology has developed, we have the means to check out anyone we hire to do anything. Sometimes, it just doesn't occur to a person who wants to hire a home care worker that being too trusting can be a costly mistake. For elders who may be more trusting than their adult children, a smiling face, friendly manner, and pleasant conversation may be enough to cause them to trust a person who applies for a home care worker job. Many a con artist and thief have the ability to fool an elder with a pleasant demeanor.

I encourage every person who wishes to bring a worker into the home to get thorough information, to do a criminal background check, as well as a job history background check. Agencies should be doing this kind of screening. If you aren't sure what an agency is doing to check their workers' backgrounds, please ask a lot of detailed questions about it.

Your elder is at risk for financial and other abuse simply because of age, and particularly, because of dementia and other conditions which affect mental ability. Many home care workers are kind, dedicated folks who enjoy taking care of elders. They enable Mom or Dad to stay at home, where most elders prefer to be, and to manage their activities of daily living safely. However, not all are honest. A home setting is unsupervised and can be very tempting for a dishonest person to take advantage of the aging person receiving care. The message is simply: beware, and if home help is needed, get it the smart way.

Carolyn L. Rosenblatt, RN, BSN, PHN, Attorney

Acknowledgments

No book can be written without inspiration from someone or something. This one is inspired by many.

Perhaps my love of being around older persons was first inspired by my wonderful grandmother, who lived her life to the fullest, staying in her home through all her declining years, until her death at age 93. She was an observer of people, and taught me to be the same, and to value what was unique in each one. Thank you, Mimi.

As a student nurse, I worked in a nursing home situated next to the nurses' dorm. It was there that I first worked with groups of aging folks. When I needed some money, I could take a shift on the weekend, and there was always work at the nursing home. I liked the work. Summers, before obtaining my license, it was the same. There was always a job available working with elders. I spent time caring for aging persons at home, in long-term care, and in the hospital where we got most of our training.

As a young public health nurse assigned to visit my clients at their homes, I discovered that I was going to be assigned a lot of "geriatrics" patients. I didn't know what to think. However, I went at it with enthusiasm. I was amazed to find out how much I enjoyed working with elders and seeing them in their own environment, rather than hospitals. The interest they had in my visits, the gratitude they showed me for the simplest thing, the true connection we made as I cared for them was a profound experience. I was fascinated, as well as inspired by how they managed, no matter what they had to overcome.

When I finally left nursing to become a lawyer (in significant part because of the limited income nurses made in those days), I left with a tear in my eye. I knew I would miss the twinkling eyes of my older folks, the smiles they gave me each home visit, and the wrinkled hands, gnarled fingers, canes, glasses, dentures and all. There was something touching about all that for me. I could never explain it exactly. I just felt at home with elders.

I acknowledge all those clients, through thousands of visits, thousands of hands I held, countless treatments I gave them, for the lessons they taught me. I am a wiser person for all the bits of wisdom they offered. Some had only one leg, some were blind, some could not speak, some had dementia, some were dying and did die, and some were just very old and frail. This book is, in part, a tribute to each and every one of them, and their families, whom I also knew. They taught me more than I could ever express.

Throughout my legal career, in which I nearly always represented injured people, I saw hundreds of clients in hundreds of difficult circumstances. Many suffered, many were disabled for a time or for good. I witnessed another dimension of human courage by being in their lives. I learned volumes from them, too. They gave me the opportunity to really see what it was like to be deprived of a way to make a living because of a disabling injury.

My job included dealing with every kind of insurance, including Medicare, Medicaid, supplemental, health, auto and disability. I learned more from those cases than I ever could have known as a nurse. I saw how hard it was for people to manage insurance problems without an advocate. I had to get evidence for and prove such intangibles as suffering, emotional injury, and partial disability. I had to delve into and articulate what it was like for the person who had lost function in a part of himself. I came to a much deeper understanding of people's lives when I had to learn so much about them, in order to effectively represent them, and to speak for them.

I dedicate this book to the many wonderful clients I served as a personal injury lawyer, as well as the patients and clients I served as a nurse. Touching their lives was a privilege that gave me another dimension. They were and are my teachers. The lessons they taught me permit me to keep helping others who are struggling with problems associated with aging.

A host of friends and colleagues helped me get this book project finished. My thanks to my fellow attorney in elder law, Eliot Lippman, Esq., who was a chapter reviewer, along with other chapter reviewers Tina Cheplick, R.N., Franza Giffen, fiduciary, Erin Winter, home care professional, and Michele Budinot, care manager. My amazing assistant Rosemarie Doherty helped me with everything, including research, and all of the mechanical aspects of production. I truly could not have done this without their help.

Finally, my thanks goes to my outstanding husband, Dr. Mikol Davis, psychologist, support team, new work partner at AgingParents.com, and patient listening ear for the last 27 years. I have the gift of a "low maintenance" husband! He is my dearest friend and beacon of light, always.

Carolyn L. Rosenblatt

Volume Two:
How to Choose a Home Care Worker

If you have noticed that your aging loved one is not managing so well on his or her own, you are probably considering getting help at home. As people age, they begin to demonstrate for us some of the signs of aging, which include loss of physical strength, memory difficulty, and the inability to keep track of things. The combination of these problems, which may or may not include disease processes such as dementia, arthritis, and other ailments, may result in a decline in independence.

It is certainly a common trait that the elder, him or herself, is not the first to recognize a decline in independence. It seems to be something we naturally resist. We do not want to admit that we cannot be completely on our own or that we are not as capable as we used to be. To do so would be to recognize that we are getting closer to the ends of our lives, and this is not something our society accepts.

In a country in which youth is highly valued, and age may be disrespected by many, the aging process and the need for help at home often meet resistance. Resistance to recognizing the need for help often comes from the elder. Sometimes, the family members also resist recognizing an elder's decline.

Facing it means facing that Mom or Dad is getting old, could be in failing health, and may die sooner rather than later. No one likes to deal with this, but the "head in the sand" approach can lead to disaster.

Perhaps on your last visit to your aging parents you discovered that the house, which was always neatly kept, has been neglected. The yard has not been tended to, nor the grass mowed. Mom's clothes are dirty, and she was always very fastidious. There is not much food in the house. Prescription medicine bottles are in disorder, and some are empty. You may have been worrying about this for some time, and you have finally come to the conclusion that is time to approach your aging loved ones with the subject of getting help.

Unfortunately, many people are in crisis when they finally start looking for a homecare worker. If you are a responsible relative, it is not smart to wait until your loved one falls at home, gets hospitalized, or you get a frantic call from a neighbor about your loved one. With some guidelines in mind, you can do the best job possible of finding a homecare worker and prevent the disasters that come from lack of planning.

Recommendations For Choosing A Home Care Worker To Assist Your Aging Loved One

The following are recommendations as to what you can do to be a good consumer.

1. *Spend some time doing research about how to locate the best care giving resource*. Failure to do adequate research and preparation can lead you to placing an incompetent worker in a loved one's home, financial or other elder abuse, or related criminal activity, and even physical assault. It may take you two or three hours to look into agencies or other resources in your community or the community where your aging loved ones reside. However, it is time that must always be spent to best honor the needs of the person you care about. Check local listings if you wish to do the hiring on your own. Talk to at least a few agencies if you wish to go through an agency to hire a homecare worker.

The pros and cons of going to an agency versus hiring someone on your own are discussed below. Remember that your elder can rapidly decline at home if the care provided to him is inadequate. Injury or financial ruin can arise from the wrong caregiver.

2. *Be involved.* If you live out of the area where your loved one resides, hire a geriatric care manager to assist you. (See *How to Find and Use a Care Manager* in this series for more information.) If you do not have the means to hire a geriatric care manager to assist you in locating the best agency for your aging loved one, look for an agency that is very communicative and has a care management aspect.

Some agency managers have no contact with the client or client's family, after the worker is placed. Other agencies have frequent contact with the client's family, the physician, social worker, and other involved persons in a "team approach." Ask about the agency's policy of being involved with the family of the elder after a worker is placed in the home.

3. *Be sure to inquire about what kind of background and qualifications check, drug screening, and what training is done by the agency before workers are hired.* Find out how much oversight and supervision the agency provides to its workers. Inquire about the frequency and method of communication with you, the person who is requesting placement of a worker in the home. Find out how long the

agency has been in business, whether it is insured, and how many people are in charge of administration.

4. *Be sure a thorough and professional needs assessment is done at the time a home worker is placed to assist your aging loved one.* Many agencies use an assessment tool, such as a checklist or questionnaire. Take a look at it, ask to see the paperwork, find out who does the assessment and their qualifications and experience in doing so.

5. *Involve the elder as much as possible in the entire process.* If your aging loved one has limited mental capacity due to Alzheimer's disease, or other dementia or conditions, their participation may be limited. However, persons in the earlier stages of dementia are still capable of participating, voicing an opinion, and providing their input. Generally, it is a mistake to simply march in and tell your aging parent what is going to happen. No one wants to lose a feeling of control over one's life. This is a critical issue.

If your loved one's mental status will allow, ask them to express their wishes, preferences, likes, and dislikes. Insofar as it is safe to do so, ask your elder to choose the right agency and the right worker.

If your elder is resistant to the idea of placing someone in his or her home, be sure that you discuss it thoroughly and well in advance of bringing an agency representative or care manager into the home. Even if your loved one refuses to choose or give an opinion, make the effort to ask him or her to do so before choosing for the elder.

6. ***Do a thorough safety inspection of the elder's home before a worker is placed there.*** Everything from removing throw rugs to reconstructing bathrooms and building ramps should be considered, depending on what the elder needs. Be sure that home care is a safe and appropriate choice for the elder rather than placement in assisted living, board and care, or other facility. If the home is unsafe, not suitable, and cannot be appropriately remodeled to accommodate the elder's changing needs, home care is not a wise choice. An elder may not be safe at home just because he or she says, "I'll never go to one of 'those places for old people.'" The deciding factor should be the elder's capability to remain there with help, while not endangering the elder.

7. ***Compare home care as a choice with other choices available to you and your elder.*** Perhaps the social isolation of remaining at home is not the best choice. On the other hand, if your aging loved one has friends and other social connections, and is able to get out to activities, home care for a time may be a perfectly reasonable option. If your elder is deprived of company, a communal living situation such as assisted living may be better and safer. Home care for an elder who is very isolated may limit social stimulation too much to be healthy for the elder.

If I Go With An Agency, What Should I Look For?

An agency should be well-established, and should be able to provide you with references. It should have a written contract or price list spelling out the charges involved and the kinds of services it can provide. If you are not sure about signing a contract, you may have it reviewed by a lawyer. However, most of the things home care agencies provide are non-medical, common sense services. It is not necessary to seek legal advice to review a service contract of this kind, unless there is any part of it about which you are confused or if the agency is unable to answer your questions. If you have any doubt, seek legal advice.

The agency should provide a thorough assessment of your elder's needs at the outset. This should include a general assessment of the elder's physical, emotional, and psychosocial needs, as well as a review of the physical environment. Safety should also be one of the major concerns the agency has as a priority.

Following an assessment, the agency should give suggestions as to what the elder's needs are as the agency has assessed them. You should be able to expect input from an agency, as their representative may be able to see things you have missed or that the elder has not told you about.

The agency should communicate with the elder's adult children or other relatives about the frequency and amount of home care they believe the elder needs. Many agency representatives have years of experience doing such assessments and they can be quite helpful to you, in making suggestions. Family members may not have a clear understanding of what the elder's needs really are. This comes from the fact that parents may not live with their adult children, that the elder may not clearly describe the problems he or she is having, and the fact that the elder's needs are probably changing as time goes by.

According to home care experts we have interviewed, about 75% of the elders served don't think they need help when it is obvious to those around them that they do. Working through the elder's resistance is the first step. One must respect the elder, yet gently push ahead, presenting the idea of help for the sake of the peace of mind of the adult child. This is an approach that often works. The elder may agree to "try it." The adult child or other relative may be able to persuade the elder to accept some help by describing that they need to have more peace of mind while they are at work or with their own families, or because they live out of the area.

Once help is in place, it is rare for the elder to reject the person who regularly comes to offer assistance. If the worker shows up each time with a kindly and respectful attitude and asks the elder what he or she would like, it can induce the elder to stick with having this help. Again, helping the elder maintain a sense of control is very important.

Elders will often tell us "I've been doing fine all by myself and I don't need any help." No one seems to be quite ready to believe that he or she needs assistance with ordinary things. However, acknowledging and honoring the elder's belief in his or her own independence, while reminding him that the adult relative or child needs reassurance that the elder is safe, can be a good approach.

What Are The Advantages And Disadvantages Of Hiring A Home Worker On Your Own?

Advantages

It is possible to hire a qualified and good home worker on your own without going through an agency. The main advantage is that you will save money. The home care business is a profit-making business, and the people who are sending workers into individual homes need to make a profit in order to stay viable. They will charge more, in most cases, than you will pay if you do not use an agency. *We recommend that you always use an agency to place a worker in your home.* We believe that the risks are not worth the relatively small cost difference of going through a reputable agency to get a competent worker to help your elder at home.

Disadvantages

There are many disadvantages to hiring someone on your own. They include these things:

1. *Lack of expertise in getting a thorough background check of a worker.*

You may not have the resources or knowledge to do a thorough screening and criminal background check. Background-checking services are available and agencies may contract for these at a reduced rate. An individual will have to spend money out of pocket, find a good background checking service, and get the information coming from the background check before hiring a helper. Without an agency, you have to do all the screening yourself. You must call references, search public records, conduct more than one interview, and the process can be daunting.

2. ***Lack of experience in screening potential workers.*** You may not have experience in screening and hiring people to do work in the home. This can be a disadvantage. People who are looking for this kind of work as a way of finding an opportunity to commit elder financial abuse may present very well, and may be congenial, experienced and warm. It is much easier to be fooled by this if you are hiring someone for the first time than if you hire people as a part of your daily business. Experienced agency employers may have developed a "nose" for the unsuitable worker. It could be that you, as an

individual, trying to hire on your own, lack the sophistication and skill to hire smart.

3. ***The Risk of Theft.*** Theft can be committed by any worker in the home. The worker is left alone with the elder for a couple of hours each day to many hours each day. Opportunities to take advantage of the situation and steal, commit identity theft, or even abuse the elder are there. Home workers are unsupervised when there is no agency involved. Individual workers not screened by agencies may be uninsured and unbonded, so you have no way to recover from a theft of money or property by an independent worker. An agency is likely to carry insurance and be bonded to protect you against loss from theft.

4. ***The need to report the worker's earnings and to withhold taxes for any employee you hire.*** According to the Internal Revenue Service, anyone who employs a private person on a regular basis at home has an employee, rather than an independent contractor. Accordingly, you, the employer, must withhold taxes according to the law, pay payroll tax, and report the earnings of your worker.

5. ***Worker's Compensation Insurance.*** If you hire a home worker, set the home worker's hours and require that they work on specific days, technically, the home worker is your employee. The rules vary from state to state with regard to what worker's compensation insurance you must purchase, but in some states it is necessary for any employee to have worker's compensation insurance as a matter of law. The workers compensation insurance premium may be something you did not plan on paying. It may be a requirement of your state's law that you have it, because workers can be injured on the job with lifting, carrying, and doing some of the many other things which elders require. Back injuries among caregivers are fairly common.

You could be liable for all medical costs for such an injury if your homecare worker, hired independently, does not have insurance to cover medical expenses in the event of injury on the job.

6. ***Unemployment Insurance.***
Unemployment insurance may also be a state requirement for any employee, even a part-time employee. Check with your local and

state laws to determine if you must purchase unemployment insurance for any worker, even a part-time worker who is employed in the home. If the worker gets fired, the worker can then collect unemployment insurance until he/she has found a replacement job. Disability insurance may also be required.

7. *The Need to Personally Check the Worker's Driving Record.* It will be necessary for you to check the driving record of any person whom you wish to either drive your elder's vehicle or who will transport your elder in their own vehicle. You will need to determine whether the worker's license is valid in your state. Most states require some form of liability insurance on the automobile that will be driven. It will be necessary for you to determine that the liability insurance policy covering either or both vehicles you expect the worker to drive is current and adequate for the vehicle and for any person injured while driving it.

Again, this can take time. An agency which screens its workers (as a qualified agency should do), will have workers ready to go when you call. The check for proper driver's license and insurance will already be done.

8. ***Independent Workers May Lack Stability.*** If you are hiring on your own, it is necessary to contemplate the possibility that the worker will suddenly quit and leave your elder without help. Workers who come from other countries may have to leave if a family member in their country of origin becomes ill or dies. The worker may get sick and be unable to work. Since one cannot necessarily anticipate such a situation in advance, you may hear, without any notice that your worker has suddenly departed for another location and you are left with no sense of when that person will return. You, as a responsible relative, can suddenly get stuck caring for your elder who has no help at home. This can interfere with your job, family, and your own responsibilities.

It is extremely difficult to find help on your own to replace a worker who departs suddenly, if your elder needs help each day. The process of background checking, checking references and the like cannot be done instantly. An agency will work to provide you with another worker as fast as they possibly can, in order to keep you as a customer.

9. ***Independent Workers May Be Unreliable in Assisting with Medications.*** Elders often have trouble keeping track of medications, keeping their prescriptions filled, and remembering when to take the medications which are prescribed for them. If an agency is involved, the agency representative or care manager can set up a system to ensure that the elder takes medicines at the proper time and in the proper amount. The agency representative can be sure that there are proper refills when the elder has run out of medication. In addition, a home worker may or may not, without supervision, be able to tell you when side effects from a medication occur, or when a medication seems to be producing a bad result.

Although many agencies do not provide licensed or highly skilled workers with any medical training, managers of the agencies who employ the caregivers can at least tell you the obvious problems that seem to be connected to the starting of a new medication, particularly if you ask for this information. If you live nearby your aging loved one and can check in on him or her each day, you can monitor the medications yourself.

If you live at some distance, and cannot be there on a daily basis, it is much more difficult to ensure that the home worker that you hired on your own will report things to you as you wish them to be reported. An agency may be more likely to provide the service of setting up a workable plan for medication assistance than an untried worker could do.

What Can I Expect From An Agency?

An agency may cost you more than trying to hire on your own, but the extra money you will need to pay an agency to find you a qualified worker is well worth it. Quality agencies are in the business of providing competent home workers. Most of the time, the home worker provides companionship services such as transporting the client to appointments, assistance with shopping and errands, reading and assistance with correspondence, purchasing of groceries, cooking and providing meals, and doing light housekeeping. The companionship services may also include reminding the elder to take medications at specific times throughout the day. For an elder with memory problems, you should not chance hiring an incompetent worker.

In addition, an agency will provide hands on care giving services such as bathing, dressing, washing hair, grooming nails, transferring from bed to chair, chair to bath, and back to bed, help with walking, and help with exercise programs. It is not what Medicare refers to as "skilled nursing." Care giving services are not provided by people who are licensed nurses or have nursing training in a formal program. It is considered unskilled or "custodial" services. Medicare does not pay for custodial services. If your elder needs a variety of custodial services, an agency will know the person best suited to meet your elder's needs.

Home care agencies will also often provide overnight shifts if elders cannot be alone at night. Most agencies will also supply workers providing the elder with care 24 hours a day. If you are attempting to hire on your own, it may be very difficult to safely find workers to cover 24-hour care. If your worker suddenly quits, an agency will supply an interim worker until a permanent replacement is found. Many agencies guarantee this service.

What you cannot expect from any agency is perfection. Workers who are carefully screened do not always meet their employer's expectations, as in any employment situation. You are responsible to make sure that your elder is safe, well cared for, and that the agency is doing its job. If you are not satisfied with what the agency has provided, it is appropriate to express your dissatisfaction, and ask for another worker. It is necessary to involve your aging loved one in the process when possible, as change can be much harder for elders than for more adaptable, younger people. Never change workers without asking your elder about it, making respectful suggestions, preparing your elder, and trying to get the elder to agree to the change.

We have been provided with a sample checklist of things to ask an agency if you are considering hiring a homecare worker. You can find It in the Appendix of this book. We recommend that you use this checklist, or one that suits your needs before you decide which agency to hire.

Do All Agencies Employ Their Caregivers?

All agencies should thoroughly screen, background check, insure, and bond every worker they provide for you, but not all home care agencies are the employers of the workers they place with you. Agencies which serve as employers for their own workers assume responsibility for payroll, taxes, insurance, invoicing your aging parent or you, and receiving payment, including checks, credit cards, or long-term care insurance, if it covers such services.

Generally, assessment by an agency representative is provided without additional charge.

Non-employer agencies, which function as placement agencies only, do not typically provide supervision of their workers, though some "placement" agencies may offer limited supervision. Ongoing supervision of workers is one of the most valuable services an employer agency, as opposed to a placement agency, can give. The agency serves as your eyes and ears. It takes responsibility for the management of the worker as well as placement.

The alternative kind of agency is a placement agency. It finds a worker, but the responsibility for what the worker does is your job to monitor. They will also screen and background check their workers, but once the employee is placed, their role ends. The employer-employee relationship is between the aging loved one, and/or their adult child, or other relative and the worker. The person responsible for the elder's money pays the workers directly, keeps track of invoices, and provides either a federally-required W-4 tax form at year's end or a 1099 tax form for independent contractors.

Placement agencies generally do not assume the employer role because there is less risk of liability, and there are fewer complications to the job of providing caregivers if the caregivers are not the agency's employees. Agencies which act as employers of the caregiver have more risk and responsibility, and more expenses than a placement-only agency.

Who Would Find Out If I Hire The Worker Myself And Don't Take Out Taxes?

If you are hiring a worker to take care of the elder in the elder's home, you set the hours and terms of work, and the worker is visiting regularly to do the job, the Internal Revenue Service considers the worker to be an employee, not an independent contractor. It is not likely that the IRS will come knocking on your door independently. It is certainly true that many people "get away with it," hiring workers in the home and never paying withholding taxes (as required by the IRS), never paying workers' compensation insurance, and never paying unemployment insurance.

However, all it takes is one disgruntled former employee to contact your state or any one of these government agencies, and you risk substantial fines for failing to comply with the law. The fines can be thousands of dollars which the IRS assesses as penalties for failure to pay the employee properly and to withhold taxes as the law requires.

Likewise, your state may require you to pay workers' compensation insurance to any full time or part time employee. If you decide to risk it and not do so, and your worker is injured, and makes a claim for workers' compensation benefits, it will then quickly become known that you have failed to provide this insurance. You can become personally liable for the cost of the worker's medical treatment, no matter how long it takes. Homeowners' insurance may or may not cover a regular employee's medical treatment.

In addition, your state may impose a fine on you if you terminate your worker, and he or she does not have the opportunity to collect unemployment insurance benefits. If your elder has the means to provide home help, or you do, this is not an area to scrimp. The elder's health and safety are at stake.

For further information concerning the responsible use of a quality home care agency, contact the National Private Duty Association. This is the first association for providers of private duty home care in the United States. Visit their website at www.PrivateDutyHomecare.org or call (317) 663-3637.

Are Home Care Agencies Licensed?

Home care agencies are not required to obtain an agency license in every state. Some states require only a business license for anyone to provide non-medical home care services in an individual's home. About half of our fifty states have standards requiring home care organizations to register or obtain a license. Because the requirements are different throughout the states, you, as a consumer, will need to determine if licenses are required in your state, and whether any agency you are considering using has the required license.

Be sure to distinguish between an ordinary business license, which anyone can get to open any kind of business, and a home care license. There is at least a greater measure of security if licenses are required in your state that a licensed agency will thoroughly screen and train its workers. Although even licensed agencies can end up with a "bad apple" of a worker, at least the screening process they normally use will improve your chances of avoiding someone with a criminal record, drug problem, poor work history or poor suitability for the job.

Ten Tips for Choosing a Good Home Care Worker

1. **Will help at home meet your aging loved one's needs?** Think over whether getting help at home is the best way to meet your aging loved one's needs. Consider all options.

2. **Do your research**. If you are going to use an agency, talk to several, ask appropriate questions, and take the time necessary to do a thorough search for the best agency you can find and afford. The Appendix at the end of this book is a good reference as to what questions to ask.

3. **Involve your aging loved one in the process of getting help**. Urge any resisting elder that you need the reassurance that he or she is safe while you are at work, or with your own family. This approach works.

4. **Be respectful and courteous**. Do not tell your elder how it is going to be or what is good for him or her. Be respectful, courteous, and ask before any decision is made. Honor the elder's need to have a feeling of control over his or her life.

5. **Use a professional caregiver agency if possible**. The risks of not doing so are tremendous. Ask questions, collect as much

information as you can, and choose an agency which provides a lot of personal contact with the elder's family.

6. **_Determine your aging loved one's needs at the outset._** Be sure a thorough assessment of your aging loved one's needs is done at the outset of getting help in the home. An objective person from an agency can see things you may miss.

7. **_Be careful at hiring on your own_**. If you hire on your own without using an agency, you need to do a complete criminal background check, drug screen, a search of public records, driving record, references, and work history check on any prospective worker. Hiring on your own is not recommended.

8. **_Is the elder driving?_** If the worker is driving a car, be sure there is adequate insurance on both the elder's car and the worker's car, as well as a clean driving record and current license.

9. **_Monitor the worker regularly._** Monitor any worker who comes into the home of your elder. Unsupervised time can lead to crimes of opportunity, whether the worker comes from an agency or not. Risk is reduced with agency supervision.

10. ***Remember to consider tax ramifications when hiring on your own***. If you hire on your own, remember that the Internal Revenue Service (IRS) considers a regular worker whose schedule you set and whose working conditions you arrange, to be your employee, not an independent contractor. You must withhold taxes, report the worker's earnings, and provide a tax form according to federal tax laws. Under state laws you may also be required to pay disability and unemployment insurance and provide worker's compensation, as well as payroll tax.

Questions to Ask When Looking for a Homecare Agency

1.   How long has your agency been in business? Can you tell me about the background of the owners/directors?   (Many new agencies are springing up because of the vastly growing elderly population. Some are opened by people who have absolutely no experience or credentials to work with this population. Longevity in the business often signals a good reputation.)

2.   What organizations in the community do you work with? (i.e. hospitals, Alzheimer's Association, Hospice, etc.) Do you have references in these organizations? Are there other references that you can give for your agency?

3.   How do you find your caregivers? What kind of experience do you require of your staff? What kind of certifications do you staff hold?

4.   *Can you tell me about the screening process they go through*? Are they background checked? Do you have them go through an orientation process? Do you have ongoing training for your staff?

5. *Is your agency employee-based or independent contractor-based?* (Very important!!!) Are taxes, insurances and worker's compensation handled by your agency? Do you pay the caregiver or do we?

6. Will someone come out to do an initial assessment? Is there a charge for that service?

7. Tell me how the scheduling works? Are there any time minimums? Do we have to commit to a certain amount of service? What if something comes up and we need to cancel, how flexible is your cancellation policy? Can we expect the same caregiver each time? Is it possible to reach an agency representative after business hours or on the weekends?

8. What is your agency's course of action if our caregiver is sick or unable to work for some reason?

9. What if we have a last minute need, can you help us?

10. What is your agency's course of action if the caregiver is not working out?

11. How do you manage your staff once you assign them?

12. How does your payroll and billing procedure work?

13. Do you offer care management? Is there a charge for those services?

14. Please tell me about insurances that your agency carries. Are your employees insured and bonded?

15. Can the staff drive? Do they drive in their own cars or can they drive my parent's vehicle? What about insurance?

16. What can I expect the caregiver to do? What can't they do?

17. What can I expect from your agency in terms of communication?

18. Does your staff keep written care logs? How often are those reviewed?

19. How often will an agency representative visit my mom or dad to check on things?

20. My mom has Long Term Care Insurance? Do you work with these policies? How much assistance will you provide in filing her claim and assuring that all the paperwork is taken care of? Will you directly bill these companies?

References

American Association of Retired Persons (AARP). 601 E Street NW, Washington, DC 20049. http://www.aarp.org.

"In-home Care for a Loved One…Will You Gamble with Your Choice of Home Care?" 941 East 86th Street, Suite 270, Indianapolis, IN 46240. http://www.privatedutyhomecare.org.

"Consumer and Worker Risks from the Use of Nurse Registries and Independent Contractor Companies," National Private Duty Association (NPDA). 941 East 86th Street, Suite 270, Indianapolis, IN 46240. http://www.privatedutyhomecare.org.

Hired Hands Homecare, Inc, 84 Galli Drive, Novato, CA, 94949.

Resources

To learn more about *The Boomer's Guide to Aging Parents* book series, and other valuable resources, see our website at AgingParents.com.

The Boomer's Guide to Aging Parents book series

How to Handle a Dangerous Older Driver

How to Choose a Home Care Worker

How to Understand the Pros and Cons of Assisted Living

How to Choose a Nursing Home

How to Find and Use a Care Manager

How to Handle Money for Aging Loved Ones

How to Handle Family Conflicts About Elders

How to Find a Good Lawyer for Mom or Dad

How to Stand Up For Your Elder in the Healthcare System

All nine volumes are available in a single, larger book, *The Boomer's Guide to Aging Parents, The Complete Guide.*

www.ingramcontent.com/pod-product-compliance
Lightning Source LLC
Chambersburg PA
CBHW071114090426

42737CB00013B/2592